MY INCREDIBLE
DINOSAUR
EXPEDITION

Written by Anita Ganeri
Illustrated by Emma Martinez

Top That Publishing
Tide Mill Way, Woodbridge, Suffolk, IP12 1AP, UK
www.imaginethat.com
Top That is an imprint of Imagine That Group Ltd
Copyright © 2023 Imagine That Group Ltd
EU Authorised Representative, Vulcan Consulting,
38/39 Fitzwilliam Square West, Dublin 2, D02 NX53, Ireland
All rights reserved
0 2 4 6 8 9 7 5 3 1
Manufactured in Guangdong, China

YOUR PREHISTORIC PASS

Your incredible prehistoric expedition starts here! With this explorer's fact book and the model in your kit, you have special access to the awesome world of long-lost creatures of sea, land and sky. This is your pass to becoming a top explorer and a prehistoric reptiles expert!

DINOSAURS AND OTHER REPTILES

Dinosaurs were **prehistoric reptiles**, but they were not the only ones! At the same time that dinosaurs were living on land, there were reptiles **swimming** in the prehistoric seas and **flying** in the prehistoric skies, too.

WHEN DID THEY LIVE?

Dinosaurs and other prehistoric reptiles lived during a time called the Mesozoic Era, which lasted from around **252 to 66 million years ago** (or 'MYA'). They did not all live at the same time, or in the same place. Scientists divide the Mesozoic into three periods: **the Triassic, Jurassic and Cretaceous**. During these times, Earth's land split from one massive supercontinent into smaller continents.

TRIASSIC PERIOD: 252 to 201 million years ago. Away from the **humid (warm and damp) coast**, the **land was hot**, dusty and dry. **Volcanoes** were common.

JURASSIC PERIOD: 201 to 145 million years ago. Inland, it became **cooler and more humid**. Lush **forests** covered much of the planet. Large **seas appeared** between the splitting land masses.

CRETACEOUS PERIOD: 145 to 66 million years ago. By now, the areas of **Earth's land had split further apart** and prehistoric **creatures evolved very differently**, in different parts of the world.

Explorer's note: Scientists have different opinions about the start and finish of the prehistoric periods and exactly when prehistoric creatures lived.

PREHISTORIC SEA, LAND AND SKY

As you head off on your expedition to discover prehistoric creatures of sea, land and sky, remember that your 'finds' often lived many millions of years apart and in different parts of the world.

IN THE SKY

Flying reptiles called **pterosaurs swooped, glided and soared** in the prehistoric skies during the Late Triassic, Jurassic and Cretaceous. They hunted for prey including insects, lizards and fish, depending on where they lived.

ON LAND

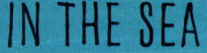

Dinosaurs ruled the land during the Triassic, Jurassic and Cretaceous periods, from hunting meat eaters, or **'carnivores'**, to huge plant eaters, or **'herbivores'**. By the Cretaceous, dinosaurs had evolved into hundreds of different species (kinds).

IN THE SEA

While the dinosaurs roamed the land, prehistoric **seas were ruled by giant, carnivorous (meat-eating) reptiles** that swam and dived in search of fish, squid and other prey, from deep oceans to shallow coastlines.

YOUR HABITAT MODEL

Your habitat model has **three tiers** — sea, land and sky. **Read the animal profile pages** and **check out the little diagram** to discover who lived where, placing each prehistoric creature in its correct habitat.

Animal models are not to scale.

SKY

LAND

SEA

NOTHOSAURUS
noth-oh-sore-us

TRIASSIC
Europe, Africa, Asia

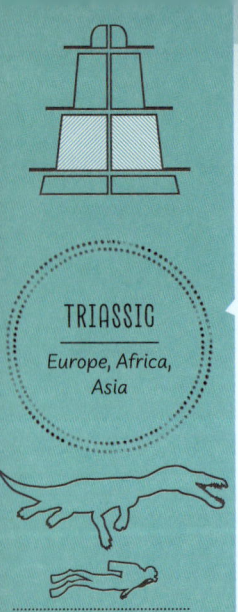

Nothosaurus was a large sea reptile which lived both in water and on land. This fierce, streamlined swimmer lived in the Triassic period.

Nothosaurus hunted for food in the sea. It may have used its **paddle-like front legs** to dig up the seabed for fish and shellfish to eat.

Like seals and sea lions today, Nothosaurus **also lived on land**. It hauled itself out of the water to rest on the shore.

It was built for swimming, with a **streamlined body, and a long tail and strong legs** to push itself through the water. It may also have had webbed feet.

Its long jaws were lined with **needle-sharp teeth**. When it snapped its mouth shut, its teeth overlapped to stop prey getting away.

Long, sharp claws on its toes helped it to grip the slippery rocks as it clambered ashore.

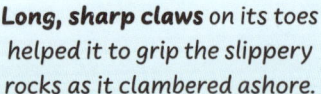

PLACODUS
plak-oh-dus

Like Nothosaurus, Placodus was a sea reptile that swam in the sea, but could also walk on land. It lived in the Triassic period.

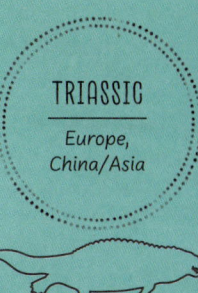

TRIASSIC

Europe, China/Asia

Placodus had a heavy, stocky body, a short neck, and a **long, flattened tail**. It used its tail like a paddle for swimming.

In the front of its mouth, it had **chisel-like teeth that stuck out**. It used them to grab molluscs, such as mussels and clams, from the seabed.

A row of **bony plates** ran down the middle of its back. Some scientists think these helped Placodus stay warm in the water, by soaking up heat from the sun.

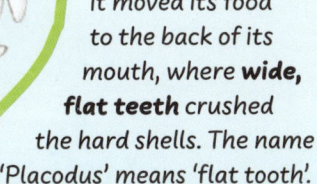

It moved its food to the back of its mouth, where **wide, flat teeth** crushed the hard shells. The name 'Placodus' means 'flat tooth'.

Its belly was covered in 'armour' of **bent-over ribs**. This might have protected it from predators. It also made it heavy so it could sink easily to the seabed to feed.

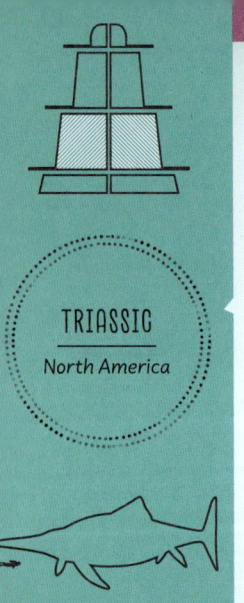

TRIASSIC
North America

SHONISAURUS
shon-ee-sore-us

Shonisaurus was a gigantic ichthyosaur — a prehistoric sea reptile shaped a bit like a modern-day dolphin. It lived in the Triassic period.

Super-sized Shonisaurus was one of the **biggest sea reptiles** that has ever lived. It could grow at least as long as a bus, and maybe even longer.

Scientists used to think it had tiny teeth and could only eat soft food, like squid. But recently, they discovered that it actually had **large, sharp teeth** for tearing into prey.

Its pointed, **beak-like snout** was longer than a modern-day human.

It was well suited to life in the sea. For swimming, it had four **long, narrow flippers** — two at the front and two at the back. It used them like paddles for pushing through the water.

Around 40 Shonisaurus **fossils** have been found in Nevada, USA. Today, the region is covered in mountains, deserts and dry grassland. But in the Triassic, it was sea.

ICHTHYOSAURUS
ik-thee-oh-sore-us

Like Shonisaurus, Ichthyosaurus was an ichthyosaur, but only a tenth of the size. It lived in seas around Europe in the Jurassic period.

JURASSIC
Europe

Ichthyosaurus was **a fast swimmer**. To power through the water, it flexed its bendy body up and down, steering with its flippers and fish-like tail.

Some **Ichthyosaurus fossils** have been found with fish bones, fish scales and tiny hooks from squid tentacles still inside their stomachs.

Its long, slim, pointed jaws were filled with **sharp, needle-like teeth** for catching fish, squid and other prey.

The name 'Ichthyosaurus' means **'fish-lizard'**.

Large eyes helped it hunt prey in murky water, and keep out of the way of hungry pliosaurs (another group of sea reptiles).

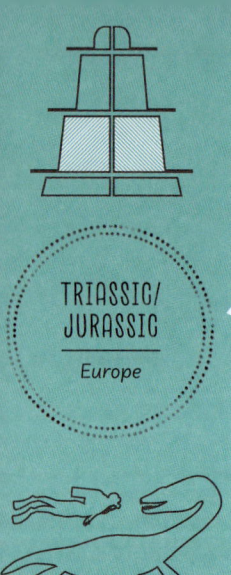

TRIASSIC/
JURASSIC
Europe

PLESIOSAURUS
pless-ee-oh-sore-us

Long-necked Plesiosaurus was a large sea reptile that hunted fish and ammonites. It lived as early as the Triassic period.

Plesiosaurus's neck was **longer than its body**, and could be swung from side to side to catch passing prey.

It had a wide, **rounded body** and a short tail.

The first complete **Plesiosaurus skeleton** was discovered in England in 1823 by famous fossil-hunter Mary Anning.

At the tip of its long neck, it had a small head and jaws, filled with **small, sharp teeth**. It could open its mouth very wide for catching prey.

Plesiosaurus had four stiff, **paddle-shaped flippers**. Like a modern-day sea lion, it 'flapped' them to push itself through the water.

LIOPLEURODON
lye-oh-plur-oh-don

Liopleurodon was a very large sea reptile and one of the fiercest hunters in the prehistoric ocean. It lived in the Jurassic period.

JURASSIC
Europe

Liopleurodon belonged to a group of sea reptiles called **pliosaurs**. They were related to plesiosaurs, but had bigger heads and shorter necks.

Its massive skull was filled with **huge, dagger-like teeth**. It had such strong jaws that it could bite large prey clean in two.

A **top predator**, it devoured fish and squid, as well as other sea reptiles, such as plesiosaurs and ichthyosaurs.

Scientists think it may have had a **strong sense of smell** for locating prey in deep, murky water.

Using its long flippers, it quickly put on a **burst of speed** if it suddenly spotted prey.

CRETACEOUS
Worldwide

MOSASAURUS
moh-sah-sore-us

Another huge, meat-eating sea reptile, Mosasaurus lived in the Cretaceous period. It ate sharks, ammonites and other sea reptiles.

Mosasaurus had a **heavily-built body**. It used its tail to drive through the water, and its flippers for steering.

The **first Mosasaurus fossils** — of skulls — were found in the 18th century. At that time, scientists thought they came from giant crocodiles or whales.

Mosasaurus may have been able to dislocate or unhinge its jaws to take a **bigger bite**.

It had **huge jaws**, lined with sharp teeth for snapping up prey. Its favourite food was ammonites — shellfish that grew up to 2 metres across.

To hunt prey, it **swam slowly above the seabed**, using the seaweed and rocks for cover. Then, when it got close enough, it attacked.

ELASMOSAURUS
el-as-moh-sore-us

Elasmosaurus was a type of plesiosaur, with one of the longest necks of any animal known. It lived in the Cretaceous period.

CRETACEOUS
North America, Asia, Europe, Australia, Antarctica

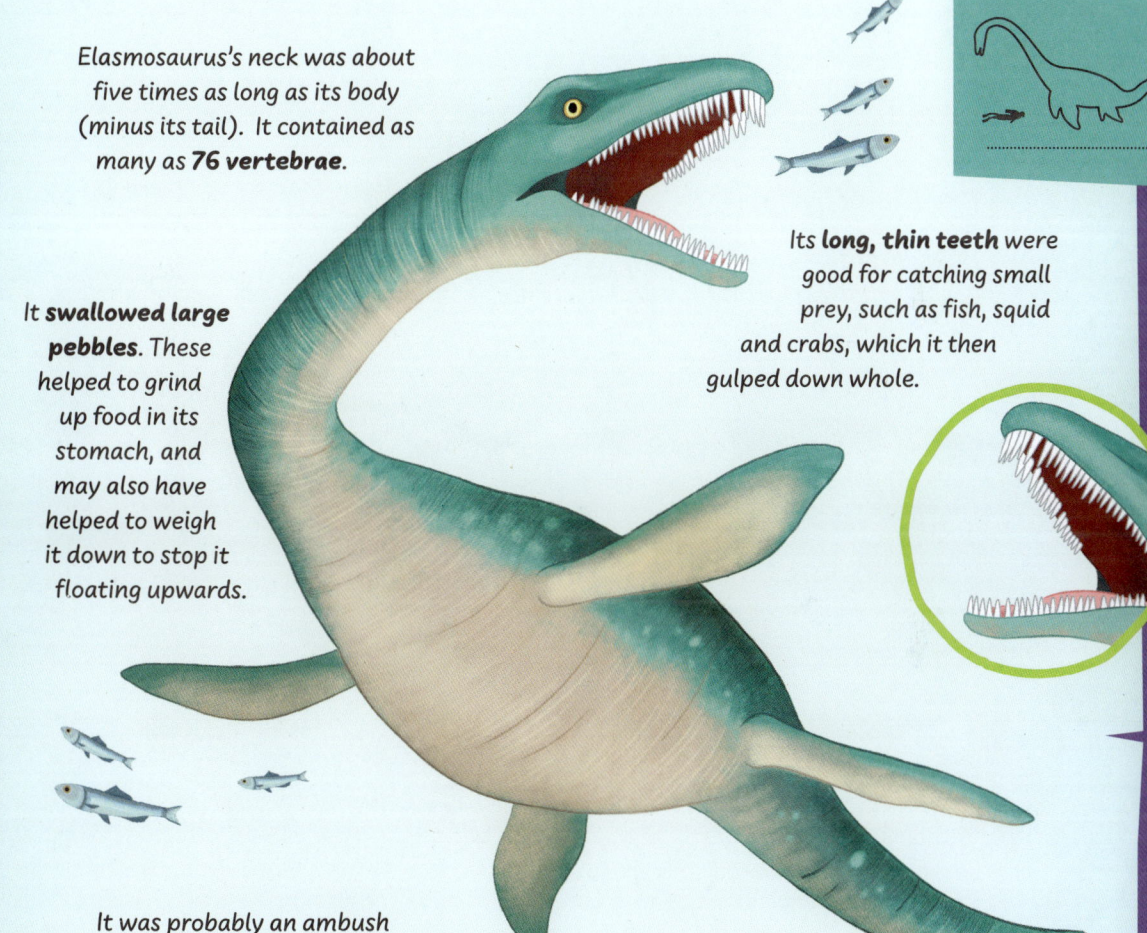

Elasmosaurus's neck was about five times as long as its body (minus its tail). It contained as many as **76 vertebrae**.

It **swallowed large pebbles**. These helped to grind up food in its stomach, and may also have helped to weigh it down to stop it floating upwards.

Its **long, thin teeth** were good for catching small prey, such as fish, squid and crabs, which it then gulped down whole.

It was probably an ambush hunter, sneaking up on a **shoal of fish**, without being noticed. Then it simply stuck its head in, and grabbed a tasty meal.

When the first Elasmosaurus fossils were found (in the 19th century), scientists mixed up its neck and tail, and put its **head at the wrong end**!

SARCOSUCHUS

sar-koh-soo-kus

CRETACEOUS
Africa, South America

Sarcosuchus was a gigantic prehistoric crocodile. It lived in rivers in what are now South America and Africa in the Early Cretaceous period, but may also have lived along the coast.

Its **massive skull** was around 2 metres long and filled with sharp, cone-shaped teeth. Its bite was strong enough to crush bones.

Sarcosuchus weighed around 8 tonnes — many times heavier than the biggest crocodile today. Its back was covered in **thick, scaly plates** of armour.

Sarcosuchus probably ate fish and shellfish. It may also have **preyed on large dinosaurs** who came down to the river to drink.

Like modern-day crocodiles, it lay still in the water, waiting for prey to come close. Then it **grabbed its victim in its jaws**, and pulled it underwater to drown.

It used special sounds to attract a mate. Scientists think the **big, knobbly bump** at the end of its snout helped make these sounds louder.

AMMONITE
ah-moh-nyte

Ammonites are sea animals, related to modern-day octopuses and squid. They swam in shallow seas around the world in the Jurassic and Cretaceous periods.

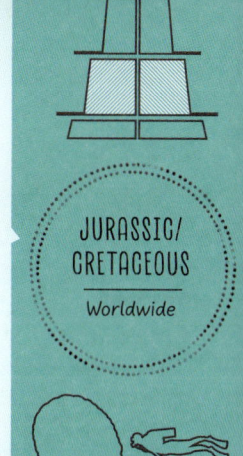

JURASSIC/ CRETACEOUS

Worldwide

Unlike squid and octopuses, ammonites had **spiral shells** around their soft bodies. They used their long tentacles to catch tiny sea creatures to eat.

They came in a **huge range of sizes** from slightly bigger than a pea to almost as long as a small car.

The shell was divided up into spaces called **'chambers'**. The ammonite lived in the last chamber. The empty chambers were filled with gas to help it float.

People used to think ammonites were coiled snakes that had been turned to stone. They called them **'snakestones'**.

Ammonites swam by squirting out water in one direction, to **jet propel** themselves in the opposite direction.

TYRANNOSAURUS REX
tie-ran-oh-sore-us rex

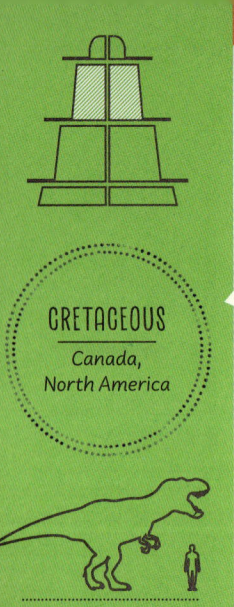

CRETACEOUS
Canada, North America

Tyrannosaurus rex, or T. rex, was a huge theropod dinosaur. One of the deadliest dinosaurs ever, it lived at the end of the Cretaceous period.

It had the **most powerful bite** of any land animal ever. Its **30-centimetre-long serrated teeth** would have made easy work of tearing flesh and crunching bone.

Tyrannosaurus rex was a top prehistoric predator. Its name means **'king of the tyrant lizards'**.

Its **short, two-fingered arms** had limited use for killing or eating, but they may have grabbed hold of prey.

T. rex's **muscular body was adapted for hunting prey** such as Triceratops and Edmontosaurus, but it also scavenged for dead animals.

This ferocious carnivore pounded across the Cretaceous landscape on its **powerful back legs** and could run up to 40 kilometres per hour.

TRICERATOPS
tri-serra-tops

Triceratops was a huge, armoured, plant-eating dinosaur. Like T. rex, it lived in the Late Cretaceous period.

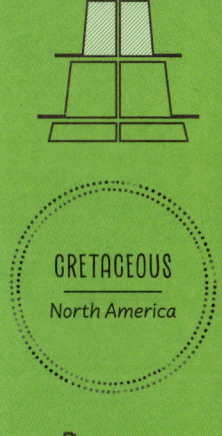

CRETACEOUS
North America

This **massive 5-tonne herbivore** would have put up a strong fight against meat-eating predators like T. rex.

The name Triceratops means **'three-horned face'**. The dinosaur's 1-metre-long sharp horns were deadly weapons for defending itself.

These dinosaurs **lived together in herds**. It was easier for a group to keep safe from predators and to protect their young, just like elephants do today.

Its neck was protected by a **huge bony frill up to 2 metres wide**, but sometimes that was not enough to keep it safe, especially from T. rex.

Triceratops's **horny beak and sharp teeth** were perfect for tearing off and eating the tough palms and cycads that grew in the Cretaceous period.

JURASSIC
North America

DIPLODOCUS
dip-low-dock-us

Gigantic, long-necked Diplodocus was a plant-eating sauropod dinosaur. It lived in the Jurassic period.

Diplodocus's **very long neck** helped it to reach its favourite tree-top leaves, low-growing ferns and water to drink.

Scientists think that it may have had **small spines** along its back.

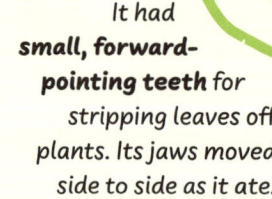

Diplodocus's **long tail could whip** backwards and forwards super-fast to make a loud noise to scare away attackers.

It had **small, forward-pointing teeth** for stripping leaves off plants. Its jaws moved side to side as it ate.

This **15-tonne Jurassic giant** did not have any natural enemies, but predators might have hunted its babies, or eaten its eggs.

STEGOSAURUS
steg-oh-sore-us

Stegosaurus was a mighty, armoured, plant-eating dinosaur. It lived in the Jurassic period.

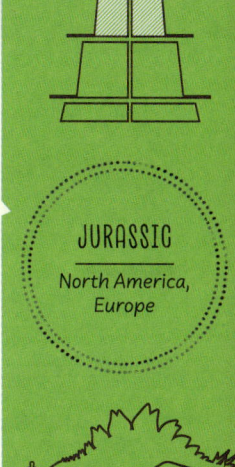

JURASSIC

North America, Europe

The **1.2-metre-long spikes** on its tail were a dangerous weapon. Look out, meat-eating Allosaurus!

The **bony plates** on Stegosaurus's back may have acted as armour. Some scientists think they could have changed colour to attract a mate or scare predators.

The name **Stegosaurus means 'roofed lizard'**, because 19th-century palaeontologists thought that its plates lay flat, like roof tiles.

It had a **head-down posture** because its front legs were shorter than its back legs.

Stegosaurus grazed on low-lying plants like ferns and mosses. It tore off leaves with its **toothless beak** and chomped them with its small, peg-like teeth.

VELOCIRAPTOR
vel-oss-ee-rap-tor

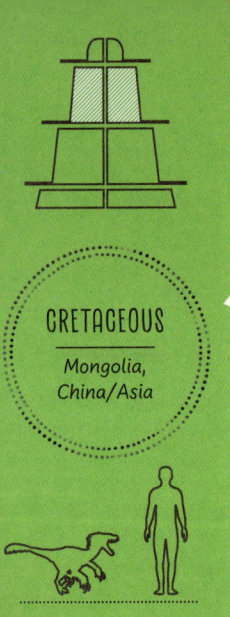

CRETACEOUS
Mongolia, China/Asia

The size of a large, modern-day turkey, Velociraptor was a deadly meat-eating dinosaur. This fierce hunter lived in the Cretaceous period.

Velociraptor was a **fierce, fast hunter**. It raced after prey on its long back legs, chasing down small mammals, lizards and even larger dinosaurs.

Like a bird, it was **covered in feathers**. But it could not fly because its arms were too short.

Its long **tail was stiffened with extra pieces of bone**. This meant it could hold its tail out for balance while it stood on one leg to attack its prey.

Velociraptor was a theropod — the same group of dinosaurs as T. rex. Theropods were the **ancestors of today's birds**.

It had long, curved **'killing claws'** on its feet which it used as lethal weapons to pin prey to the ground. Then it tore it apart with its sharp, jagged teeth.

PACHYCEPHALOSAURUS
pack-ee-kef-ah-lo-sore-us

Pachycephalosaurus was a sturdy plant-eating dinosaur, famous for its big, bony head. It lived in the Cretaceous period.

CRETACEOUS
Canada, North America

Pachycephalosaurus's skull was an incredible **25 centimetres thick**, with a thick dome on top. More bony lumps and spikes covered its snout and neck.

Scientists once thought it used its hard skull to headbutt rivals, but it is more likely that the dome was for showing off to **attract a mate**.

It had a **beak-like mouth** for grazing on plants, seeds and fruit that grew in its warm, humid habitat. But it may also have eaten insects — we don't know for sure.

Despite **its bulky body**, Pachycephalosaurus could run quite fast on its strong back legs, holding its long, stiff tail out to help it balance.

Some scientists think the dome may have been **covered in skin** that was brightly-coloured or could change colour.

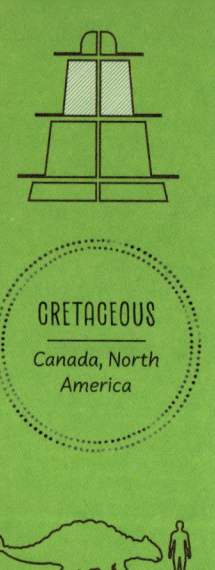

CRETACEOUS
Canada, North America

ANKYLOSAURUS
an-kie-loh-sore-us

A huge, armoured dinosaur, Ankylosaurus was built like a tank. It lived in the Cretaceous period.

Its **long, clubbed tail** was a deadly weapon. If an attacker got too close, Ankylosaurus swung its tail around and broke its bones.

Its body was covered in hard, **bony plates, knobs and spikes**. This armour protected it from attack by meat eaters, such as T. rex.

Its wide, triangular head was heavily armoured, with horns sticking out from the top and sides. It even had **bony eyelids** to protect its eyes.

Ankylosaurus's only weak spot was its **soft underbelly**. So, an attacker would have to flip it over to kill it — a tall order, even for a T. rex.

Ankylosaurus had a squat, **low-slung body**, and four short but incredibly strong legs to support its massive weight, between 4.8 to 8 tonnes!

SPINOSAURUS

spine-oh-sore-us

Spinosaurus was an enormous theropod, longer and heavier than T. rex. It lived near the coast in the Cretaceous period.

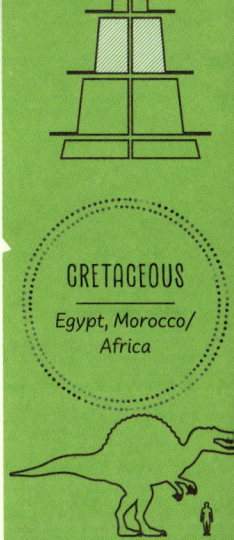

CRETACEOUS

Egypt, Morocco/ Africa

Spinosaurus lived in places that were once **mudflats and mangrove swamps**. It may have spent most of its time in the water, or along the shore.

It had a **spectacular 'sail'**, around 1.5 metres high. The sail was made from long spines growing from its back.

Its **nostrils were high up on its head**, close to its eyes. This may have helped it breathe while it lay in the water, waiting for prey.

Scientists aren't sure **what the sail was used for**. It may have helped cool down Spinosaurus's body, attract a mate, or even propel it through the water.

Its long, narrow jaws were filled with **smooth, cone-shaped teeth**, ideal for catching fish, even if these fish were 3 metres long!

PARASAUROLOPHUS
pa-ra-sore-oh-lof-us

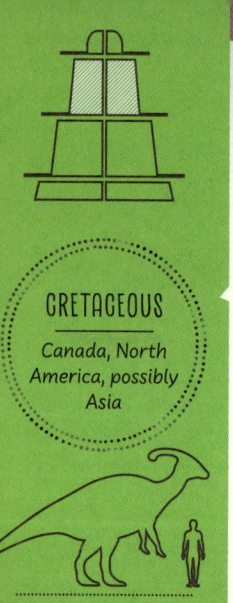

CRETACEOUS
Canada, North America, possibly Asia

Parasaurolophus was a hadrosaur (duck-billed dinosaur). Famous for its fancy headgear, it lived in the Cretaceous period.

Several duck-billed dinosaurs had **big, bony crests** on their heads. At 1 metre long, Parasaurolophus's was the longest and strangest.

Its crest was a **long, hollow tube** that curved up and backwards from its skull.

Today, scientists think the head crest worked like a trombone that **blasted out alarm calls** to keep the herd together and warn of predators.

A plant eater, Parasaurolopholus **probably spent most of the day foraging** for food on all fours. But if danger threatened, it could sprint off on its back legs.

It **lived in large herds** which may have provided more safety. A herd moving suddenly would have confused an attacker.

PTERODACTYLUS
terr-oh-dak-til-us

Pterodactylus was a crow-sized pterosaur — a prehistoric flying reptile. It would have been spotted in Jurassic skies.

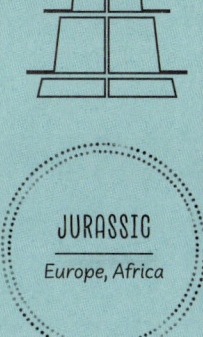

JURASSIC

Europe, Africa

Pterodactylus's wings were made from thin layers of skin and muscle. They stretched from its extra-long fourth finger to its back legs. Its name means **'winged finger'**.

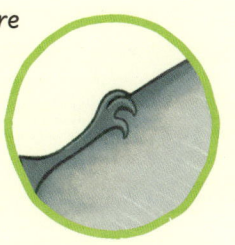

When the **first Pterodactylus fossils** were found in the late 18th century, scientists thought they belonged to a sea reptile that used its flippers as wings, to fly.

From **fossil tracks**, scientists know it could also walk on land. It walked upright, on all fours, with its wings folded up.

It had a **long, narrow skull** with lots of cone-shaped teeth. It probably ate small animals, insects and fish, as it walked along the shore.

The **small, soft crest** on its head was mostly used to attract a mate. As a young Pterodactylus grew into an adult, its crest grew bigger.

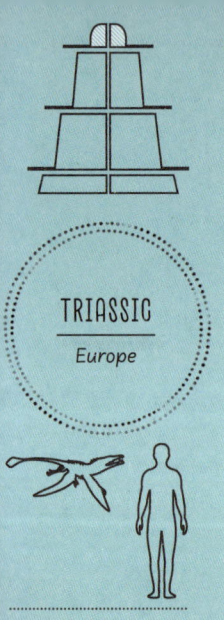

TRIASSIC
Europe

EUDIMORPHODON
yoo-dee-morf-oh-don

Eudimorphodon was a small pterosaur, and one of the earliest pterosaurs known. It lived in the Triassic period.

Eudimorphodon had **typical pterosaur wings**, stretched between its long fourth fingers and its back legs.

Its long, bony tail may have had a **diamond-shaped flap** at the end. Scientists are not sure what the flap was for. It may have helped with steering in the air.

Until 1973, no one had heard of Eudimorphodon. Then, scientists in Italy discovered **a nearly complete skeleton**.

Pterosaur teeth were usually simple cones, but Eudimorphodon had several different sorts. At the front were large, needle-like teeth, with lots of smaller, multi-pointed teeth behind.

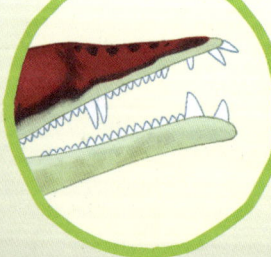

Its jaws were only around 6 centimetres long but were packed with more than 100 teeth. It probably ate a **diet of fish, insects and shellfish**.

PTERANODON
terr-an-oh-don

One of the best-known pterosaurs, long-winged Pteranodon was also one of the largest. It lived in the Cretaceous period.

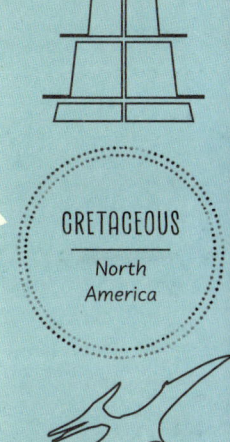

CRETACEOUS
North America

Pteranodon had **very long wings**. It might have flown like a modern-day albatross, soaring for long distances over the sea.

Its massive skull was longer than its body and ended with a **very long, pointed beak**. It did not have teeth, but used its sharp beak for catching fish and squid.

The **large bony crest** on its head may have been used for attracting a mate. It may also have been brightly-coloured.

Like all pterosaurs, **it had fur**. Hair-like strands covered its body and part of its wings.

Scientists know it ate fish because **fish bones and scales** have been found inside the stomachs of Pteranodon fossils.

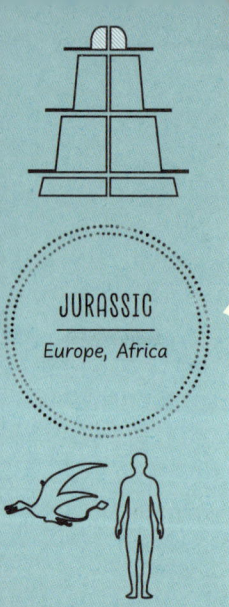

JURASSIC
Europe, Africa

RHAMPHORHYNCHUS
ram-for-in-kus

Rhamphorhynchus was a seagull-sized, fish-eating pterosaur with very long wings. It lived in the Jurassic period.

Rhamphorhynchus had a long skull with a sharp, curved beak. Its beak was filled with **needle-like teeth** that slanted forward and meshed together to grip prey.

It most likely **snatched fish** as it skimmed over the water. In turn, it was hunted by fast-swimming prehistoric fish.

Some scientists think Rhamphorhynchus **hunted for food at night**.

More than 1,000 **Rhamphorhynchus fossils** have been found, from whole skeletons to teeth, and even poo. One of the most exciting finds was of a wing.

At the end of its long tail, it had a **diamond-shaped flap** which may have been used as a rudder to steer in the air.

DIMORPHODON
die-morf-oh-don

Dimorphodon was a medium-sized pterosaur, famous for its large, boxy head. It lived in the Jurassic period.

JURASSIC
Europe

Dimorphodon's head was **huge for the size of its body**, but large openings in the skull bones meant it was surprisingly light.

Compared to other pterosaurs, it had short wings and was not a strong flier. It was better at **walking on all fours** and climbing trees.

It probably only took to the air as a last resort to **escape from predators**. Its long, stiff tail may have helped it to balance.

From studying Dimorphodon teeth, scientists think it is more likely to have eaten **small lizards and mammals** than insects or fish.

Its name means **'two shapes of tooth'** because it had two types of teeth in its jaws. Long, pointed teeth grew at the front with shorter, flatter ones at the back.

QUETZALCOATLUS
ket-zal-kwat-lus

CRETACEOUS
North America

One of the largest flying animals ever, Quetzalcoatlus was a gigantic pterosaur. It lived in the Cretaceous period.

With a **wingspan the same as a small plane**, Quetzalcoatlus would have had to jump around 2.5 metres into the air, then flap to take off.

Like a modern-day heron, it used its **long, sharp beak** to pluck fish and other small animals from rivers and streams. With **no teeth**, it swallowed its prey whole.

Despite its huge size, its body was **extremely light**. In the air, its broad wings meant it could soar enormous distances without needing to flap.

It stood as **tall as a modern-day giraffe** when it was on the ground.

On land, it **folded its wings up and walked on its back legs**. Its wings were so long they touched the ground, so it had to be careful not to trip up.

QUICK QUIZ

What can you remember from your prehistoric expedition? Try answering these quick-fire questions to see if you have achieved 'expert' level.

Which prehistoric sea reptile had one of the longest necks of any animal known?

Which spiral-shelled sea creature was a relation of today's octopuses and squid?

Which prehistoric predator was 'king of the tyrant lizards'?

Which fierce, speedy hunter is known for its long, curved 'killing claws'?

Which plant-eating dinosaur had a head crowned with a thick, bony dome?

Which coast-dwelling dinosaur had a spectacular spiny 'sail' on its back?

Which gigantic pterosaur was one of the largest flying creatures ever? (You are definitely an expert if you can spell its name, too!)

USEFUL WORDS

These are a few of the words that are useful for a prehistoric explorer to know.

Carnivore: an animal that eats meat

Continent: a large land mass on Earth's surface surrounded by sea

Cycad: a palm tree-like plant with cones (similar to fir cones)

Fossil: the remains or impression of a prehistoric plant or animal embedded and preserved in rock

Hadrosaur: a large, plant-eating Cretaceous dinosaur with flattened jaws, that mostly walked on two legs

Herbivore: an animal that only eats plants

Ichthyosaur: a prehistoric sea reptile similar to today's dolphin, with a long, pointed head, four flippers and a vertical tail

Mesozoic: the prehistoric era that is divided into the Triassic, Jurassic and Cretaceous periods

Palaeontologist: someone who studies fossils to learn about the history of life on Earth

Plesiosaur: a prehistoric sea reptile with a broad, flat body, large paddle-shaped limbs, a long, flexible neck and small head

Pliosaur: a kind of plesiosaur with a short neck, large head and massive tooth-filled jaws

Predator: an animal that hunts, kills and eats another animal

Pterosaur: a prehistoric flying reptile with wings made of thin layers of skin supported by an extra-long fourth finger

Reptile: a cold-blooded animal that produces eggs and uses the sun's heat to keep its blood warm

Sauropod: a huge plant-eating dinosaur with a long neck and tail, that walked on all four legs

Theropod: a meat-eating dinosaur that walked on its back legs and had short front legs

Vertebrae: small bones that form an animal's spine